RHYTHM OF LIFE

AN ANTHOLOGY OF POEMS
VOLUME-IV

RAMESH CHANDRA PRADHANI

Dedicated to

All the poetry lovers,

Readers and worshippers

Believers and appreciators,

Messengers and Narrators,

Fonders and creaters,

Searchers and researchers,

Discoverers and inventors,

and above all, explorers of literature

having enthusiasm and inquisitiveness .

Contents

Preface   *xi*

Acknowledgements   *xiii*

Prologue   *xv*

1. Grain-growers   1

2. Words As Wizards   2

3. Cross Roads Of Life   3

4. Speechless Speech   4

5. Poetaster   5

6. Poetic Brook   6

7. It All Started With Tears   7

8. Purposeful Living   8

9. Valentine's Day Experience   9

10. Taming The Tongue   10

11. Miracle   11

12. Penitence   12

13. The Best Teacher   13

14. Poetic Lust   14

15. Overload   15

16. My Mask   16

17. Real Warrior   17

18. Dearth Vs Aspiration   18

19. My Art My Light   19

20. Wanderlust   20

21. Karma - Maker Of Character   21

22. Books   22

23. You Before Me   23

Contents

24. Dreams Are Doorways   24

25. Shooting Star   25

26. Gone Are Days   26

27. Quote Poem   27

28. Quote Poem   28

29. Magic Of Endurance   29

30. One Day You Will Come   30

31. Spiritual   31

32. Solitary Life   32

33. A Poison Tree   33

34. The Courageous Loser   34

35. Mother's Kiss   35

36. Disgust   36

37. Cradle Of Life   37

38. Tears Of The Sea   38

39. Underwhelm   39

40. War Is Not A Solution   40

41. No One Is Ugly   41

42. Violence, A Weapon Of Ruin   42

43. Quote Poem   43

44. Merry Christmas Day   44

45. Pleasure Of Freedom   45

46. Life Goes On   46

47. True Heroes Never Die   47

48. Unconditional Love   48

49. Money   49

Contents

50. Life Does Not Exist Alone ... 50

51. The Oldest Language Of The Universe ... 51

52. Guru Is Guru ... 52

53. Quote Poem ... 53

54. Quote Poem ... 54

55. Love Is Not Enough ... 55

56. Woman Power ... 56

57. Inhuman Actions ... 57

58. Quote Poem ... 58

59. Say Not Them Labourers ... 59

60. Despotism ... 61

61. Lunatics, Lovers And Poets ... 63

62. We Can Win ... 64

63. Building A Better Nation ... 65

64. Pray God To Make Us Rich ... 66

65. Birth Of Sri Ram ... 68

66. Affection ... 69

67. Warriors Against Corona ... 70

68. Happiness Potion ... 71

69. The Path ... 72

70. Sleep ... 73

71. Inside Out ... 74

72. Existence ... 75

73. Rumination ... 77

74. Her Unknown Destiny ... 78

75. Life Without You ... 80

Contents

76. Crying In The Rain   81

77. Service Begets Peace   82

78. Truth Triumphs At Last   83

79. The Ideal Family   84

80. Coming Back Vs Setting Back   85

81. If You Stop Trying   86

82. You Can   87

83. My Youth Days   88

84. Revenge   89

85. Job   90

86. Being Alone Is Not Easy   91

87. Kindness Can Change Lives   92

88. Repeated Mistakes   93

89. Can't Hurt Me   94

90. Why We Do   95

91. Built To Serve   96

92. Win The Day   97

93. Love Rules   98

94. Success Is Sum Of Small Efforts   99

95. Mistakes Are Opportunities   100

96. National Energy Conservation Day   101

97. Silence   102

98. Pray, Trust, Wait   103

99. Change Is Necessary   104

100. Be Free, Be True, Be You   105

101. Never Be An Option   106

Contents

102. Everything Has Its Own Time 107

103. Listen To Your Heart 108

104. Some Losses Set You Free 109

105. Life Without Action 110

106. Some Souls Suffer Silently 111

107. Pleasure And Freedom For Pain 112

108. Listener 113

109. Push Yourself 114

110. Less Ego, More Soul 115

111. Be Nice, But Learn To Say No 116

112. Protect My Energy 117

113. Accept The Situation 118

114. My Failures 119

115. Don't Quit 120

116. Sometimes Some Moments 121

117. Be Kind To Yourself 122

118. Patience And Motivation 123

119. Ego 124

120. Discipline 125

121. Meditation 126

122. Murky Seren Night 127

123. Tough Situations 128

124. Try Again Better 129

125. Time Is Powerful 130

Preface

With the passage of time everything changes its place and position emulating the competitive world of sophistication and victory. With the growth and development of civilazation human being takes his pleasure to explore the world with his inate instint and wants to conquer the whole world knowing his span of life, that is, quite transitory. Nevertheless, he incessantly makes his journey towards the destination. On the way he has to face so many challenges, some are easy and some are risky, some times with frequent failures, unavoidable circumstances and problems as a result of which he is supposed to be faded and disapppointed. As life is not a bed of roses for all, it is diferent from person to person and place to place. However, life is to move and grow amidst all adversities- physical, mental, economic, religious, cultural and conjugal etc. .

In such a critical juncture a person needs help, consolation and motivation to recover from his helplessness and disappoinment to march forward. The present anthology of poems"Rhythm of Life" Vol-IV brings with unending source of stimulation experiencing sweetness of the intermingling of pain and pleasure in life. Moreover, it also traverses through the ups and downs of life so as to forage self confidence, hope, faith and perseverance- the needs of the time that provides a happiness potion to all the avid readers of poetry. The anthology serves as a tonic to revitalize and to recuperat the voracious readers from their mental depression and hallucination.

Ramesh Chandra Pradhani

Acknowledgements

All the poems in the anthology deals with variety of themes on human, his nature and behaviour, symphony of human feelings-love, hatred, anger, revenge and many more. Some of poems are from the core of my heart and some are from outside natural objects and social happenings. It's my great pleasure and oppurtunities to cumulate such impressive and heart touching poems written from time to time and bring them out into a book form under the title" Rhythm of Life", An anthology of poems Vol-IV which could not be possible without the support of my family and their inspiration.

In such a moment of rapture i extend my humble gratitude to the publisher of Notion Press, Chennai and the entire team involved in this remarkable work for bringing out the publication of the anthology in time.

My gratefulness to my friend Durbadal Ghibela, Reader in English in Jarasingha Higher Secondary School, Jarasingha in the district of Balangir in Odisha(India), who unconditionaly extended his helping hands in publishing the anthology.

I am also thankfull to Bimal kathar, an expert in typing, who whole heartedly supported me for the preparation of manuscript of the anthology.

Ramesh Chandra Pradhani

Prologue

" THE RHYTHM OF LIFE" is the rhythm of my life

Containing one hundred and twenty five Poems of many types

Dealing with diverse thems on human lifes and nature vibes

Creating a rhythm in life, mesmerising myriads of mind

Life dances in the waves of melodious songs of love and life of its kinds.

"THE RHYTHM OF LIFE" replete with magic and music

Readers in euphoria become so energetic and dynamic

The can build the edifice of love and harmony, cosmic

keeping in mind the value of poetry which makes them poetic.

Each poem of this anthology is like a pearl of life

Having a look on it takes away all human strife

Reading poetry makes you laugh and cry with a purpose

Let the life be meaningful chanting the song in chorous.

Ramesh Chandra Pradhani

1. Grain-Growers

•

A man of simplicity full of humility, peace and tranquility
Deeds are common but thoughts uncommon, a man of solidarity.
May be poor in prosperity but not in dignity
Lack of complicacy and conspiracy, a man of magnanimity.
A man of painstaking, tolerance and perseverance
Life savior of millions with firm confidence.
A real hero playing with soil and water
Growing grains in life does something better.
Sad is his lot who always meets loss and loss
Nevertheless, runs not away from purpose.
Might be a poet, thinker, politician or administrator
Time and luck, but, compel them to be cultivators.
Think of if the world is dearth of grains growers
What would happen to the mankind in entire universe?

2. Words As Wizards

• 2 •

Much more than wizards sweet words to hypnotize
The frenzied avengers to cool down otherwise.
Even when mothers utterly fail to sympathize
Makes the stubborn baby sleep in disguise.
The best weapon the mankind to socialize
Makes the people laugh sorrows to minimize.
For the irrecoverable loss to realize
Makes the notorious cry to penalize.

3. Cross Roads Of Life

· 3 ·

Life a mixture of crossroads of pain and pleasure
Amalgam of ups and downs nobody can eraser.
Sometimes smooth and sometimes rough
Bewildered to follow, undecided the tough.
The simple and short cut may lead to adversity
But painful and struggling life crests all calamities.
Must we take time to decide the best?
Consequences be dangerous if chosen in haste.

4. Speechless Speech

Each heart a speaker of speechless speech
The deep sea speaks about the sea beach.
Audible the speechless speech of eyes
Impressive what body language says to rise.
Crying of a child mother can understand
And smiling face makes her so jocund.
Chirping of nestlings expresses feelings of appetite
Mother birds cannot stay out of their sight.
The letters of touch the blind can read
Hearing of sounds a ray of light can lead.
The mute can perceive the language of gesture
No problem to follow any kind of stricture.
When there's no obstacle
Silence makes miracle.

5. Poetaster

At the first step a child can't stand alone
What it needs is support with loving tone.
Time takes to be refined and strengthened
With falling and rising gradually gets enabled.
Nobody or nothing wholly perfect
Feelings emotions experience steadily inject.
The mind and heart with several aspects
That stimulates in a way to what others expect.
Encouragement and motivation makes one march forward
Underestimation and negligence pulls backward.

6. Poetic Brook

From core of heart rises the poetic brook
Falls in the vast ocean of mankind troop.
Passes through lanes by lanes of society high and low
Poor and rich, love and hate, birth and death follow.
Hills of criticism, plain of recognition stands before me
Flow never stops over day and night however gloomy.
Accompanied by many a rivulets of thoughts and emotions
Breadth dilated length elongated with lore of prediction.
Unlike the mundane stream no current of passion shriveled
The more it runs the more flooded with fructuous land.
Everybody's thirst quenched each appetite suppressed
The steady burble of running water alleviates the oppressed.
Never ending swirls sweep away solitude of solitary wanderer
A chance happens to shape the future of characters.
Eternal is the poetic brook
Neither molested not squeezed by hook or crook.

7. It All Started With Tears

Happy was family jocund were parents and children
Time passed away in merriment when all was in vain.
It all started with tears when they got married
And tied with the knot of nuptial bond so hurried.
Just after few days sons and daughters left homes
Peace and pleasure of which once the epitome.
The poor parents lying in bed pondered over their absence
What a mystery of creation they wondered in deep silence.
Died the helpless couple inside home together
Everything lost before came to know the neighbors.
Their relatives informed but could not reach in time
However sad finished the funeral rituals by locality with rhymes.

8. Purposeful Living

Living with a purpose makes life tremendous
To find out the underlying truth of cosmos
Incorporated in every particle in abundance
Let life be quite useful towards people benevolence.
Living with a purpose makes life meaningful
For no negativity piercing the heart forceful
Life is a series of actions to render
If purposeful nothing or nobody can hinder.
Living without a purpose seeming harmful to all
In spite of a beautiful gift above all
Responsible for invitation to the downfall
However life is amalgam of rise and fall.

9. Valentine's Day Experience

Love is not made
Love becomes natural
When mingled two souls
Whole as a part and part as a whole
A pledge forever
If you do what you love
And love what you do
No matter it's whatever
Comes with flying colors
All endeavors
No ponder, nothing measure
Gap of age, wealth or race
If whole heartedly embrace.

10. Taming The Tongue

A unit of test to taste sweet or sour
Gauge the flame of pepper ensure
A tool to speak the hidden truth like monarch
Help taking food into the store of stomach.
Unhealthy situation may occur when tongue slips
Friends become enemy with a flip
Dare foes be turned into bosom with clip?
Brave is he who can tame the tongue
Worshiped everywhere for long as song
Utterances of words depends on the person
He must think the impact before any action.
Anger can provoke the tongue to do the wrong
Words once uttered never comes back along
Self control is medicine to calm down
The stupidity of tongue the fire one can put down.

11. Miracle

Nine months pain gives a mother divine peace
A mould of blood in her womb now comes to exist.
A calf jumps and walks after a few hours of birth
Rushes to the shed with its mother in mirth.
An owl can see her prey in quite deep darkness
A bat can eat and call for nature through mouth.
Moving of Earth around the sun never stops
A stone throwing over sky returns back and falls
Trees bearing fruits on their branches on time
More than reality and miracle, mere sublime.
Everything is a miracle in its own place
All miracles occur due to God's grace.

12. Penitence

Human life a mixture of actions and reactions
Having both good and bad deeds, though no intention.
More delighted with more well service in silence
So, be not hesitant to have more penitence.
Penitence not a matter of hatred or vice
Rather one of the best spices of life.
Positive attitude leads to humble gratitude
Let penitence be a right and fine substitute.
Life having no penitence, one sided
Without mouth no poem be recited.
Penitence, unlike perfume, remain unfaded
If you take it whole heartedly or embedded.

13. The Best Teacher

There is love where there's life
Life teaches the mankind how to survive
And love, on the other hand, how to revive
Song of love- a universal vibe.
Love gives patience and courage to wait
Four lettered word no one can measure the weight.
Like a tree loaded with fruits so humble
Makes one stand, however many a times stumble.
The twin flames of love sacrifice and devotion
Refines the love of heart with perfection
Strive to embrace the divine emotions
Can behold and read the words in motion.
A screw to join the two legs of a compass
To clear traffic, a bridge to connect the bypass
A signboard to show the right path to destination
The best teacher to train mankind in all situations.

14. Poetic Lust

Curiosity to explore the unknown makes me mad
Slumber lost in loneliness to see ahead.
Get relaxed when something expressed
For the depressed soul often suppressed.
Take pleasure searching rarity of things inside
The moment ultimate bliss of mine comes outside.
Closer to the divinity I approached with poetic lust
Without which no fire of creation outbursts.

15. Overload

Everything or everybody has its own size and space
To stay anywhere anytime any moment to face.
The way the creator thinks to create fully justified
To balance the law of nature necessarily rectified.
Much expectations results in loss of success
Greediness ultimately looses the race.
Too much of words, too much thoughts damage one's image
Too much of anything- the source of ruining self courage with knowledge.
Time never supports the man out of track
As if the spirit of luck enthusiastically remained slack.
The key to development gets junked before to open the gate
To repent over the matter to cope it is too late.

16. My Mask

• 16 •

Everybody masked with a mask of selfishness of own
Inside which hides the devil of callousness, groan.
Inside something and outside something to play
The game of masquerades, somewhere to display.
Humanity is at stake beneath the mask
You are the answer and you are the questions to ask.
Everybody inside the mask heartily wants to bask
For the sake of humanity, no need to wear a mask.

17. Real Warrior

Cancer fighter real warrior of the Tim
Without being tired lifelong fighting to survive.
Let's come forward to give them moral support
That will enable them to drive away remote.
However fatal stand together to defeat
Surely we can remain aloof from the culprit.
Nothing to worry nothing to hurry if precautions taken early
Rise and fall, fall and rise inevitable for mankind mingled purely.
Let's enrich ourselves with the food of prevention
That will kill cancer forever without hesitation.

18. Dearth Vs Aspiration

Dearth a desert of despair
Aspiration Ocean of desire.
Dearth of wealth makes one poor but honest
Desire for wealth delights but engulfs the rest.
Undermined the dearth of commonsense
Does miracle, though, talk nonsense?
Dynamic are people in senses kill humanity
Threatened the future of mankind in stability.
Dearth of freedom seeks liberty, unity and fraternity
Sacrificing self, greed, pretence and proclivity.
Aspiration for achieving target crests culmination
By opting any means of corruption.

19. My Art My Light

Every creation is an art big or small
Devotion and commitment as a whole.
Enlightens some hearts more or less
Reforms and reshapes with peace or solace.
Light that removes the darkness
Smile to shine the pale faces with freshness.
Guiding star that shows the unknown path to the passerby
Destination comes closer to the eyes.
A flicker of hope to stand for adversity
A source of inspiration for facing any calamity.
Courage to encourage the defeated soldiers
Promises to fight against enemies' enclosure.

20. Wanderlust

Makes things around us familiar
Nothing remains ever peculiar
As experience teaches informal
Still more valuable than formal
Lore after wander practical.
The world a vast book a classic
Earth the upper cover fantastic
How beautiful to look hypnotic
Sky being the lower, erotic
Adds the pleasure aesthetic.
To wander is to read avidly
Pages of each episode vividly
Must we strive to heed lucidly
To watch every anecdote gladly
Like sumptuous food to feed.
Dawn to dusky twilight
Sunrise to sunset
Full of wanderlust
Things known perfect
If you are really lost.

21. Karma - Maker Of Character

Some are great by birth, by fate
Some by deeds, destination in quest
Karma with righteousness opens the gate
With love, dedication mould better the best
Popular are the both wrong and right doers
In respective domain of action and reaction
The right continues to exist for long
But the wrong vanished like water bubble
The fragrance of karma spreads all over
Remains unfaded, imperishable to move farther.
Charm of karma magical for the honest
Taste of karma sweeter for the committed
Patience, perseverance the tonic to glaze
The color of karma, steadiness and selflessness adds to blaze.
Bad karma never spared its owners
Whereas good one passes to all others
Mortals be immortal in the realm of extinction
Death never comes to those duty lovers
But the habitual wrong doers die each day being clever.

22. Books

Civilizations may fall and rise

Monuments, temples get destroyed

River can dry forest can fly

Books are the imperishable wealth of mankind

Neither be stoled nor be ruined

Mortals are left immortalized behind

Let's plough the land of books with the tractor of reading

The scope of minds is fertile to yield harvesting

The master piece of universal wisdom

As long as the world exists

Will stand a new kingdom

Where humanity only subsists.

23. You Before Me

• 23 •

You before me a lively goddess to worship
Materialization but cuts our blood relationship
An image of Kindness Ocean of fondness present me before
It's beyond my imagination to perceive your lore
Before me you stands as a mountain ranger
To check the current of mishaps forces of danger
My selfishness makes me blind to see thy presence
That always guides me saves me from impotence
You before me a torch to torch the path to destination
A milestone of stimulation to give me mirth of progression
A blessing in disguise to reach me final target
Besides love affection never seen anger or hate
That's your divinity blessed with grace
Enables me to win hard to harder any tough race.
You before me my strength, stamina solace and spices of my life
Never before never after ever have I felt human strife.

24. Dreams Are Doorways

• 24 •

Dreams born with life grow and end with life
Like shadow unseen, untouched but loyal to advice
Like bodyguard stands for safeguarding its master
Caters the needs, makes the haven with booster.
Seeing dreams is discerning doorways to future
Without dreams life is weaker to culture
The best of the things, very often nurture
Reshapes the destiny committed enrapture.
Each dream a stair of ladder to reach the pinnacle
Once is started the journey, remains not any obstacle.

25. Shooting Star

A shooting star is a falling star a meteor
Appears to be fallen on Earth's corner.
A symbol of positivity, a well wisher
King of flashing lights, maker of lovers.
Avid reader of inner heart, a foreteller
Giver of blessings, solace, patience, a true caller.
Being fallen you show the bouquet of dreams
All possible hopes and faith shower on them.
Thy presence ascertains the God's existence
Dreamers are assured with full confidence.
A beholder intently beholds with great charm
Surmising that there is no harm.
Since time immemorial existed in the people's mind
Life of lives reborn when you leave behind.

26. Gone Are Days

Rains come and go but leaving a show
Summer arrives and passes offering a glow
Spring appears but disappears with flow
Without ruins nothing can take the lead to grow.
Days after days, nights after nights pass
Something legs behind, something does surpass.
But unforgotten are some truly encompass
Things passed may not be a moss.

27. Quote Poem

Poetry and sorrow twin sisters born from a mother
Poet is their father and mother together
Literature their family pleasure the brother
Where sisters happily reside with others
Having a special place of their own
Win the hearts of readers and writers in the domain
Poetry is where sorrow exists
Sorrow is where poetry subsists
Different in nature always stand together
Purpose is the same to sensuously please
Messaging the mankind universally teach
Everything goes smoothly without a hitch.
(Poetry Is The Sister Of Sorrow- Marce-Andre Fleury)

28. Quote Poem

•28•

Melancholy, suffering, calamity or any adversity
Opens the windows of heart for solidarity
Emotions soar in the firmament of tranquility
To take away the garbage of worries and anxiety.
Effervescent hearts betray not, to sing songs of pulchritude
Muses of divine bliss sprout from heart in multitude
Like the wind, can appeal the whole mankind
Leaving truth of pain in joy and joy in pain behind.
Enthusiastically ploughs the land of both love and hate
Mingles sweetness and bitterness to nourish one's fate.
Chariot of poetry flies with wings of twin flames
Fueled by love to admire and hatred to blame.
(Poetry.. the clear expression of mixed feelings-WH Auden)

29. Magic Of Endurance

• 29 •

Each moment of life faces a challenge

Intensity of scorching sun, heart shaking coldness

Deep dark of dilemma in failure and success

But there's a magic in endurance

Essence of life lies in perseverance

Pain is inevitable however evanescent

Forbearance doorways to the destination though straitened

Opens the gate of fortune for the tolerant.

The path of journey not always straight or smooth

Some portion thorny and snaky, some flowery

Brave hearts are those who march forward, smell the fragrance of

glory

Endurance endears to embrace the patient and the plucky

The charm behind every affliction makes man lucky

Hardship and inconvenience never let them be spooky

Fruits of tolerance enrich the hearts with cozy future

Turning all tears to smiles with a flicker of hope to rapture.

30. One Day You Will Come

Let me hover like clouds in the sky
Pouring the showers of rain
The peacocks on the earth in quest of me
Dancing and singing vigorously then.
Let me flow like a bubbling river
Sailing like a boat
Till the advent of the sailor
Let me float.
Let me bloom like flowers
Spreading fragrance each hour
Let me stay in the garden of your heart
Unless you come will never depart.
Sanguine of God and ultimately you to play
One day you will come
Sweet are the uses of waiting and delay
Unshakeable faith I have on the outcome.

31. Spiritual

Nobody born to be called spiritual
Actions beyond physical make spiritual
Changes are obviously natural.
Thoughts unhampered to humanity
Deeds not detrimental to solidarity
A bridge to the gap of diversity
Immortal souls to the end of divinity
Lies beyond human capacity.
Plans scheduled for the worldwide unity
Voices raised for the safety of rights and equity
Humanitarian attitude for the secularity
Justice, equality, freedom and fraternity.
Beyond mundane perplexity.
Steps taken for establishing peace, harmony
Moments of universality observing ceremony
All lead to calm down human cacophony
With the music and melody of symphony.

32. Solitary Life

A gifted life graced with fearless mind

Ease and comfort can never bind

Nor the obstreperous hullabaloo of towners

Can muddle the contemplated thoughts of solitary owner.

A searcher of jewels of rapture in the core of solitariness

A far sighted visionary to discern the advent of newness

Magnanimity in simplicity and nobility in uncommonness

And often uncommonness in the heart of commonness.

Not a curse rather a blessing in disguise

Underlying truth of nature to visualize

The whole universe dances under his feet

Who once blessed to greet the Almighty's feet?

33. A Poison Tree

• 33 •

Hidden emotions unless expressed
Turns to be a poison tree to be graced
Grows inside the core of heart
Without being able to come out.
Let the emotions flow outside massive
Share it to friends and relatives to gossip
Let the heart be fully relaxed
To allow something more to refresh
Suppress not the emotions excess
Save yourself from its oppression for recess
Hidden Emotions just like your own knife
Nobody can say at what time it may take life.

34. The Courageous Loser

• 34 •

Loser is not a loser unless destroyed
Just a failure to garner courage to stand.
Meets his visage of negligence
To be inspired by patience and perseverance.
Loser is not a Loser keeping on fight
Defeat or victory not a matter to excite.
Lose is to gain something to revive
Struggle is the real means to survive.
Life a circle of beginning and end together
But loss or profit not the end either.
Be the fighter till last breath
Worry not about what is truth of death.
Think not the loser as coward
Whimsicality offers the reward.
Brave is he who never cares for result
In his life never waits for a halt.

35. Mother's Kiss

• 35 •

Spell of magic a jocund comic

Healing powers ambrosia showers

An escutcheon for my arms during fight

A helmet to safeguard my head while on bike

Girdles me with the fence of motherhood

Her caress for me a waterproof and a fireproof.

Clothes in a robe fully bulletproof.

Ointment for attenuating ailments

Flowers blooming on my pavements

Omen of blessings in disguise

In every situation I can poise

What I am I can vehemently realize

Certainly mother's kiss my divine bliss

What makes the difference, a moral being?

Warmth of love, juice of compassion, mother's kiss

In the land of my heart pullulates the bud of peace?

36. Disgust

What I like most
Detested by others
Because they love
Stealthily as lovers.
A mental state of mind
Very often reminds
Nature of humans
Strangely hides inside.
It wonders how to alter
A man of divine character
Searching within or
Outside contactor.

37. Cradle Of Life

• 37 •

Life sways in the swing of joy
Just like a glittering toy
If things taken light to enjoy
Light heart enlivens being gay.
Every life has something fabulous
Narrated by the people garrulous
God's grace fulfills the purpose
Accepted blessings seem marvelous.
The rope of the cradle lies in His hand
No worries before we comprehend
Swinging may take time to stop
Let not go the desired thoughts flop.
Let not the cradle be ever dwindled
No one or no possession be swindled
Something we are bestowed to handle
Every situation must we mandle.

38. Tears Of The Sea

Sips her tears silently speechless
Preserved inside heart calmness fearless
When natural calamities shake her backbone
Undone unspeakably helpless to groan.
Insensibility of humans adds her sorrows harmful
With their inhuman actions to and fro shameful
Enwrapped her purity in the blanket of poison
Serenity and sanctity mudded with soil erosion.
Sea the heart of worldwide rivers, stream and drains
Mingled to the mother's lap of vastness with disdains
Can't dry the tears of magnanimous sea
As they are the carriers of human's recklessness.
Everything has a limit of its own to mildly endure
After crossing the lining bar nobody can ensure
What will happen at what time nothing can ascertain
Compelled to give birth the offspring of deadly cyclone.

39. Underwhelm

Sweet words never comes out in anger
Users of rough language are sentiment monger
Who blindly passes comments sharper?
Than the edge of a knife that may cut own finger.
Distance makes a gap of understanding
Carefree, tension free in thinking and doing
Bad or good not at all a matter of introspecting
The consequence of what one wishes.
Near and dear, bosom friends even family underwhelmed
By negativity, monopoly and excess haughtiness dwelled
Actions or reactions congenial to ambience always suits
No disappointments engulf but let anyone to pluck the fruits.
Silence instead often allures for the quest of novelty
Leave not others be underwhelmed by your ingenuity
Better to remain away from superficiality
The reason of mistaken embellishment in purity.

40. War Is Not A Solution

• 40 •

Humans are emulative by nature
Never remains stagnant rather hanker
After money and power to tower
Here and there to erect the skyscrapers.
For fulfillment of self can go any extent
Never think of relations in present
Devalued before the earthly materials
Bubbling pleasure of temporariness supposed to be real.
Wrong deeds multiplied to the height of limitlessness
When in no way wish to go back from selfishness
Pride and vanity makes them blind to see or feel the consequence
Invites the war to conquer all in advances.
Ultimately the ways they adopt push them to the hell of war
Lives, wealth name fame smashed in the fire of rushing war

41. No One Is Ugly

Ugliness a part of the Almighty's creation
With a purpose of balancing nature and emotion
Ugly things pave the way of divine beauty
World of disparity in seeing and thinking a beauty
Outside not exactly what inside reveals?
The good only exist for the evils.
Dark is much awaited to have light
Tomorrow is not what today's appetite
The blank be filled with something trifling
Stupidity sometimes does mind- blowing
Think not what you see is always right
Inside which lies truth and beauty of foresight.

42. Violence, A Weapon Of Ruin

Easy to make a violence to ruin
Lives, property, name fame nothing to win
Selflessness when provoked to flame
Throwing mud each other to blame.
Envy, jealousy and desires unfulfilled leading violence
Cutting branches on which sitting in silence
Insensibility, animalism fires at humanity
Forgetting the glorious past of maturity.
Violence ignites the force of nastism and autism
Stops stopping the flow of advancement in humanism
Wise to be far away from madding crowd
To prevent nourishing the root of sadism.

43. Quote Poem

Hidden are some words more poetic than poetry
Enormously please heart that never wishes to quit
Making mind more enthusiastic, tasks to complete
Words worthy of magic if closely sought.
Vividness and lucidity the soul of expression to tempt
Makes readers avid and esoteric, from all adversity to exempt
Wit, fun, conceit and reason with embedded irony
Together glorifies the language of symphony.
Language carries what the speaker delivers
And the way it moves to the mass his caliber.
Spontaneity of thoughts and feelings makes a difference
Poetry is the first and last for better preference.
(Always be a poet even in prose-Charles Baudelaire)

44. Merry Christmas Day

• 44 •

Happy Christmas Day to reserve
Happy happy birthday to observe
To Lord Jesus Christ His day
The Messiha of peace to say.
A day of celebrating simplicity
Hope of the hopeless in reality
Eyes of the blind to see Almighty
Sense of the senseless, agility
A day of remembering the deific advent
Light of the world to illuminate the innocent
Saviour of liberating souls immanent
Replanting the seeds of love inherent
Featherless but fearless angel to alight
As Santa, seraphic children to delight
Darkness of the whole universe to ignite
To quench thirst, to subdue acute appetite
Offering salvation, reshaping civilization
Suppression of oppression, alleviation of subjugation
Essence of humanitarian, credence preservation
Intuition of Time, conveyance of unification.

45. Pleasure Of Freedom

• 45 •

Feeling free and frank to ride
Heart enlivens inside to excite
To fill the blank outside
Nothing in vain if sure to provide.
Unloaded are the load to light
With a ticket to board the flight
Change the life's mode right
Rosy the travelling road wide.
Heart gets enlightened
Scope of mind widened
Future looks brightened
Ambition heightened.
Free mind can free yourself
Seal not your inner self
Let freedom be thy pelf
Stay blessed and safe.
Taste of freedom quite sweet
Lit the lamp of enlightenment
To emancipate pure senses
Winning all sort of huddles race.

46. Life Goes On

Life is living during a fixed period
But never stops growing or moving on
Let not try to block the way even or odd
Strive to cope with positive hope, never abandon
Let life consume what it needs
It is your duty to take proper heed
Unchain the inner self to rid
Nourish yourself others to feed
Life is for giving and taking
Each part or each moment of life stimulating
Ignore not, delay not, protect for sharing
Life is for life to live and work inspiring
Life ends where it starts creating a circle of time
Turning and turning it never fades to entwine
Joys and sorrows, high and low as food or wines
But takes something to survive in fugitive mine.
Life goes and comes, germinates to grow
Life fattens, heightens, widens and augments to flow
Marching forward and onward piling some memories to glow
Slow and steady lives wind the race of time without blow.

47. True Heroes Never Die

• 47 •

Heros are they who never quit
Always strive to remain fit
Facing challenges boldly to defeat
Slackness, negativity, impossibility making unfit.
Real heros never leg behind
Duty their religion being so kind
A worshipper of actions not of words
Incessant love and devotion supersedes.
True heros triumph over effort not over victory
Defeat is vanquished creating mystery
For their loyalty, integrity breaks record of history.
Heros men of toil and soil care for nothing
Everything bows head before his patience and perseverance
They more or less do something innovating
By adopting the weapons of tolerance.
Real heroes never die even after death
Assumed as if had taken a little bit of rest
Remain alive their heroic deeds in everybody's mind and heart
Unforgettable heroism they can never depart.

48. Unconditional Love

For a mother no one is ugly
As the epitome of unconditional love
Both bad and good treated equally
Mother's lap really an angelic hub.
An understanding no one can have
Rather than a mother
Sacrifices, dedication selflessness adding intensity
An icon of tolerance, perseverance with sanctity.
Devoid of expectations, imposition by heart
Anger full of love never even think to hurt
Caring and sharing the elements of love
How can one emotionally rob and rub?
For a mother home is heaven
Family her life meticulously weaved
With color of love having no condition
Fulfillment of divinity, serenity, might and creation.
Mother's love unconditional love no one can define
More she loves, more her love gets refined
Like diamond unconditional love always shine
Magic, music, melody, potion, blessings and nector enshrined.

49. Money

Hankering after money
Steals away one's sleep
Whoever takes the journey?
On the way to goal he slips.
Money mercilessly kills humanity
Relatives' friends near and dear
Root of socio-economic calamity
Moneyed men never ever endear.
Money makes deceptive conditions
Stands on fragile foundation
Multiplies unwanted tension
Matters not desired solutions.
Money is just something
That does not win anything
But without having money
One can do nothing and nothing
More money more greed
Selfishness always breeds.

50. Life Does Not Exist Alone

Life never ever remains alone
Foolish to enjoy life without cyclone
Of ups and downs, pangs and pain
The entrance of springs shuts down
Without summers, winters and rains.
Life can never laugh with open heart
Without shedding tears
The more tolerant, the more jubilant
The more patient, more vibrant
Life grows out of helplessness like a phoenix
Emerges like cheese or ghee out of milk losing own existence.
Life never sways in the swing of peace and happiness
Unless it falls, gets injury, suffers in calmness.
Life does not exist alone
It stands upon the foundation
Of love, affection and humanity
On the pillars of faith, hope and loyalty
Amidst the rains, wind, dust, dew drops, sun
Mending, moulding, reshaping humans to run
On the way towards destination.

51. The Oldest Language Of The Universe

If there's any language the oldest one
That's the poetry one can say
Since time immemorial people express
Inner feelings to someone in silence
Sometimes they chimed in rhymes
With the passage of time
It takes to diverse kinds
The easiest one to employ for expression
Entering into the heart of millions
Can win the several minds of depression
With the texture and mixture of poetry
Opens the gate of all mystery.

52. Guru Is Guru

A common man of epoch-making uncommonness
A simple man of sacredness and large-heartedness
Whose duty enlightened with nobility and humility
A man of reformation, revitalization coverage
A man of transporting the goods of knowledge
Being a rover, ranger, changer to unleash savages
A transformer of electric insightful privilege to give mileage
Guru is he who can teach, preach, sermonizing inner instinct
Who can hammer, batter and cater the needs succinct
Who can furnish, accomplish tasks of urgency in integrity
He is really deserving to be a guru of mankind in equity
Guru is he who motivates, translates, emulates in prudence
Well equipped, well established and enriched with self confidence
Guru is truth, nonviolence and equality
Guru is power, courage knowledge and wisdom fraternity
Guru is hope, faith, trust, light and excitement
Guru is joy, happiness, peace, harmony and embankment
Guru is blessings, Guru is curse to balance
Guru is cool, hot, liquid, solid and multifaceted forms in glance
Guru is the vast ocean of stability so deep and dense
Like massive banyan tree offers shades of solace
GURU is daylight, sunlight, and moonlight at starry night pervading
Worldwide, ups and downs, high and low, plain stretching
Guru is religion, science, and philosophy, full of, rhymes
Refiner, re-shaper, nourisher, re-builder of innovative chymes.

53. Quote Poem

• 53 •

Every ending has a beginning to start again

But every beginning has no end to finish gain

Desire is unlimited to finish the measurement

Life may ruin but incomplete is the journey to amusement.

Poetry the ladder to the limitless sky of creativity

A sojourn of life to get refreshed with sublime integrity

Aeroplane of life alight to leave for destination

On the way, often dashed with bad weather of location.

Like the hair of human head never finished growing

Like the water of cascade never stops flowing

But runs through even the crevices of stone and soil

Poetry waits not, wants not anybody to rejoice.

(A poem is never finished, only abandoned - Poul Velary)

54. Quote Poem

• 54 •

Poetry a matter of emotions coming out of heart
The first of its genre to express feelings or experience.
Newborn baby in mother's arm gives ears to mom's lullaby
That mesmerizes and makes them sleep thereby.
Mother busy inside kitchen croons the rhyme of chimes
Drudgery of toil, sweat and soil lessened with holy hymns.
Pain captivated, pleasure revitalized with blink of eyes bounced
When mothers sit before the altar reciting slokas for worship.
Farmers start singing while ploughing land with couple of bullocks
More merrily during homecoming when sun sets behind hillocks.
While departing Kith and kin the brides sobbing in rhymes
Helps melting the hearts of vast gathering.
(Poetry is the mother tongue of the human race - JG Hamann)

55. Love Is Not Enough

Love is not enough unless you feel
Love is sacrifice spontaneously heal.
Love is not enough unless you share
Love is natural nobody can stop to dare.
Love is not enough unless you care
Love is blind to see things right bare.
Love is not enough unless you understand
Love is innocent however pure in its stand.
Love is not enough unless you bear
Love like light shines to cheer.
Love is not enough unless you free
Love gives away everything like a tree.
Love is not enough unless you respect
Love is unconditional, anything never expects.

56. Woman Power

No creation possible without women
Men are incomplete in their absence
Women fill the gap of men
But men cannot without their presence.
Women the embodiment of power
Versatile enough in character and nature
Diverse roles they can simultaneously play
They are the source of strength born to display.
Women the backbone of society
So priceless and lovely gift of Almighty
Committed are they to render the revered service
Lifelong fighters for sustaining peace
Reservoir of understanding to handle the situation
Enriched with magnanimity tempted to compassion
Habituated with family management can steer the nation
Women's empowerment paves better administration.
Women in all the plinth of the race
Ocean of love and kindness divinely graced
Respect her, worship her and heartily embrace
Stream of sacredness washes away distress from all faces.

57. Inhuman Actions

Neither poverty nor suffering hereditary
For some curse for some blessings but momentary
Fate destined to suffer due to inhuman actions
The child left accursed not accountable to situations.
The world spacious enough to accommodate
Childhood the stage of ignorance to update
Forget to be a beholder, let's inundate
All our pride and vanity before receiving a mandate.
Join hands to clean the filth of abhorrence
Time to prove the purpose of life's essence
Having faith in abundance with credence
Make your presence effulgent in someone's absence.

58. Quote Poem

The very substance of the ambitious is merely the shadow of a dream
Life without ambition is like empty vessel's scream
Planets and satellites gyrate on the axis already fixed
No chance of colliding each other or they twist
Ambitions make timetable for life to accomplish tasks
Reasons of basking to catapult the target
How can a passenger ride the superfast express without a stoppage?
The ambitious in advance book their tickets for safe passage.
Man of ambition is man of expedition
Solid and successful in every action
Nobody can grab my shadow from my ambition
That's the only means to reach me destination.
(The very substance of the ambitious is merely the shadow of a
dream- Shakespeare)

59. Say Not Them Labourers

Say not them labourers who are makers of the edifice of happiness

No rains, no sun in any season prohibit them from demonstrating aptness

Wooden objects and structures beautifully shaped in the hands of carpenters

Bloomed like flowers in different colours of sweetness

Say not them labourers who are the builders of the palace of peace and pleasure

Laying the foundation of strength, stability, stamina with hard labour of gleasure

Committed workers of stone and metal by callings named as sculptors

Make the stone lively that can seem laugh or cry in the eyes of visitors

Say not them labourers who are the architect of temples, churches, masques,houses, buildings, roads and bridges

Without any glitches, clitches, crevices engraved with the heart touching artistic beauty of aesthetic images.

Say not them labourers who are the painters of human desires, hopes, wishes and expectations

Drawn with brushes of experience, coloured with the hues of emotion, final touch with power of dedication

Say not them labourers who are the jointers of broken pieces of attraction

Connectors of tears and smiles, light and heavy load of construction

Say not them labourers who are the true lovers, worshippers and
forerunners of labour
The real enrapturer, enwraper of the world neighbors.
Say not them labourers who are the reservoir of will power,
constructive liking, and courage
Vanquish all huddles, obstacles overcoming mirage
Open heart creatures are they to accept one and all without
knowledge
Hand and head strong men of mountainous magnanimity to face any
challenge.
Say not them labourers who are the cultivators of land to yield crops
and vegetables to feed
Whose punctuality, sincere duty, patience, perseverance and efforts
always take our heed?
How helpless are we to exist without the kindness of the rustics
Just think of the role of farmers in our life in closing eyes and you will
stop underestimating.

60. Despotism

Destructive power destroys humanistic power of love, peace and
harmony to enjoy transient merriment

Desert of soft, tender, purposeful life suffocating like fish out of water
in dearth of life giving element

End of democracy shrinks the realm of humanitarianism, socialism
and fraternity

Era of despotism leading to the demise of equality, justice, loyalty and
integrity

Selling of humanity in the market of butchery, conspiracy, monopoly
and terror

Skyscraping the tower of cadaver enwrapping in the blanket of cold
blood and horror

Power seeker, lover of regicide, matricide, fratricide, worshipper of
malafide intention

Poisonous and contagion are the noble patriotism, brotherhood and
sisterhood in the dungeon of despotic exploitation

Onset of animalistic barbarism throwing the trap of slavery, loneliness
and uncountable stories forever untold

Onerous are the tasks of murdering faith, hope with the weapon of
treachery unbearable to load

Tyranny overrules the ethics of time, place, person in thoughts and
actions with benevolent service

Terrific are the dreams of future, sunrise, hills, valleys, forest, and
mountains in the cacophony of injustice

Unspeakable are the annals of suffering, obscure are the colours of
mornings, nights prevails with unending gloom
Inevitable loss of nature, relations, near and dear, flowery bunches of
friendship in the garden of cruelty never bloom.
Sucking blood by force, torturing innocent lives, harbouring the ships
of jealousy are game of hide and seek
Sans realizing, repentance, crude consequences of the players of
despotism they be severely sick
Manipulating the ages of innocence, sanctity of socialization, honesty
of simplicity,
Made the edifice of despotism on the foundation of heartlessness but
never lasts long in the holy land of the Almighty.

61. Lunatics, Lovers And Poets

Poets are great lovers of prolific expression
Silent are they to roam in the firmament of imagination
Speak to own self words in motion
In quest of love, peace, harmony, prime ambition.
All lovers are lunatic in action and reaction
Hovering in the sky of deep meditation
Blind to the world of materialism to see the destination
Forget them in the solitude of concentration.
Lunatics, lovers and poets uncommon, though unreal to the common
Belong to the same world of fantasy, hub of composition
In their dreams preserved something unique recreation
Emulous rapture they derive in reshaping the existing world.

62. We Can Win

Be sure nobody is your enemy
Just try to find out the alchemy
The so called enemy was once a fast company
A partner in life's cacophony and symphony.
Sweet, soft and supportive words in talking
Remain not aloof from him in responding
Forget not to help him or her in time of acute need
Instead of their unwillingness in thoughts or deed
You see the snow of acrimony will slowly melt away
And the dirt of misunderstanding is washed away.
Be the savior of life in someone's peril
To be the only one unforgettable and unavoidable zephyr.
In no time, we can win the heart of our enemy
With the weapon of love, sympathy and harmony.
Yes, we can win; we can win one and all
Only when we stand for someone's rise and fall.

63. Building A Better Nation

Each individual, more or less a builder of the nation
Hence all are equally responsible to the construction and the
destruction.
Common man to elite person, peon to administrator
Employee- employer, daily wages worker to even prime minister.
Executive, legislative, judiciary and media the pillars of the nation
Where loyalty, honesty, and integrity of individual make the stern
foundation
The edifice of a nation stands on the pillars, and the pillars on the
foundation
If anyone of the all loses strength, sure is the devastation.
Delay in service, treatment, and maintenance invites inevitable
dislocation
Delay in execution, legislation or justice opens the gate of corruption
Unless the root of manipulation is completely out
No poison tree of desires for luxury and comfort dried off.
Partiality, monopoly, indiscrimination in any action
Like burning fire spreads here and there in shape of reaction
Undoubtedly shakes the backbone of nation
Like slow poison it may deactivate the smooth function.
Steps to be taken to reward the good and culprits be punished
Let the people know their limitations not to languish
Joining hands for the betterment can only vanquish
All hindrances of the path of development, then a better nation are
established.

64. Pray God To Make Us Rich

Praying God in diverse forms a common phenomena among
humanness
Men and women tend to visit the holy places of blessedness
Some for siblings-son in priority, some for amassing property
Some for power to emulate in name, fame and identity.
Are not they the slaves under selfishness poisonous to humanity?
Are not they betrayers to betray the Creator butchering posterity?
But now is the time, pray God to make all of us rich than the richest
Rich in heart, a heart free, frank and fair to greet one and all to accept
Rich in positive mind to think the goodness of His creation without
distaste.
Surmising introspect, deeply concentrated to proof the just of
interest.
Rich in sweet, soft words to smile the aching heart morn to sunset
Passing unhurt, winning uncontested that will not let others make
upset.
Rich in actions noble than the noblest, heavy than the heaviest
That will shine in the darkness of mundaneness brighter than the
brightest.
Rich in thoughts higher than the highest, wider than the widest
Enables us to subdue the narrowness of ignorance with zeal and zest.
Rich in empathy, sympathy and telepathy to read others' emotions to
respect
And share the feelings; treat the healings faster than the fastest.

Rich in believing ourselves, in accomplishing assignments
Loyalty, integrity, responsibility adds to fulfill commitments.

• 67 •

65. Birth Of Sri Ram

A creation of an age for someone's salvage
Something to save from the damage
Genesis of an age to pay heartfelt homage
For the courage to vanquish the savage
For the salvation from the materialistic bondage.
Embodiment of God in the form of His beloved human
The cherished dreams of the epoch to attain
Love, peace, harmony, fraternity and unity to sustain
To free the earth from the servitude of the demon.
Sacrifice of luxury for welfare of the subjects
Worshipper of deific fatherhood without any object
Staunch believer in pally brotherhood without any suspect
Treatment of women as the goddess of highness and respect.
Incarnation of tolerance, perseverance and confidence
Image of affection, compassion, credence and reticence
Epitome of sanctity, equity, solidarity in essence
Icon of divinity, sacredness, maturity in silence.

66. Affection

O Lord, give me hands of iron to check the smack of anger
And heart of steel to prohibit the gale of ensuing danger
That insensible human, in life, who sow in the land of purity
The seeds of hatred and malice to grow to spoil unity
The erotic desires to rape by force blindly, the teenagers
The daredevil dreams to build the castle of avengers
The bad will to be emulous to smash many a likes
To push them into the dungeon of dislikes.
All I need to suppress with thy benign grace
If am equipped with iron hands and steel heart
I will, definitely, gladly, for humanity, embrace.
By rendering something good, then only I can depart.
Shower upon me the rains of affection
I can flood the earth of violence and retaliation
With the fertile soil of love, peace, compassion
Myriads of plants of solidarity for production
Make me a blacksmith with a gift of anvil
To burn and blow, to reshape the future of humanity in peril.

67. Warriors Against Corona

Doctors, nurses and health workers inside kit day and night
War footing treatment sacrificing life, often overnight.
Police personnel, fire brigadiers, rovers rangers without rest in luxury
Fully committed, shouldering responsibility, over corona, for victory.
Social workers more conscious helping the helpless, homeless
wanderers
Assuaging appetite, quenching thirst, offering masks with sanitizer.
Anganwadi and ASHA workers extending helping hands door to door
Created awareness in people insiders or outsiders, rich or poor.
Politicians, Sarapanch, members, administrators held together to fight
the pandemic
To drive away the contagion from the land of majestic.
Army, Navy, Air forces heartfelt dedication vanquished Corona
Families of the deceased truly honored warriors for their stamina.
People abiding Corona guidelines, captivated at home to bear
Stopped roaming outside praying the saviour out of fear.
Working class people losing livelihood and valuable lives
Staying far away children from parents, husband's from wives.
Writers, poets, thinkers, journalists, educationists, NGOs all joined
hands
Some directly, some indirectly contributed in various form.
Some in words of advice, some in action in disguise
Each one rendered something more or less for Corona to fight.

68. Happiness Potion

Belief in yourself before believing others
Change yourself before changing others
Control of desires, staying under senses
Makes one satisfy in all cases
Be pleased with the present the real
Dreaming too excess quite unreal
To gallop everything is surreal
The way you nurture your life
The way you behave
Enriched with what you feed
Same way comes the response
Reaction results of action
Happiness a state of mind to expose
Our mind just like a bell
Echoed when is beaten
So happiness not always lies in happiness
And sorrows not in sorrows
Each one the potion of other
Both are complementary to each other
Happiness must come after suffering
And sure suffering after happiness
No-one separate two entities
Imbalance be the nature
If you dream one without the other.

69. The Path

The path of life not easy to travel
Neither straight nor smooth
Some slippery, some thorny
Certain path we have to choose
If taken the flowery one
Destination we have to loose
Rosy road be followed by the roughest one
And the other by the former
Difficult path makes one bold enough to proceed
However disappointed paves for the unknown
What we need a friend of hope and confidence
In ourselves, the way be not long to walk along
Goalpost discerned after the clouds of adversity dispensed
It is the difficult path that always makes difference.

70. Sleep

O, smoothest Sleep
But for you I would be really mad
It is for you a rosy bed are made
Day long worries can never hurt me
Nothing remains to be gloomy
A crazy companion to share all
Till I deeply asleep fall
Every night I die too born afresh
In the lap of unconscious darkness
O my life partner the watcher of my life
Unless you come, laugh at me all my strife.
Heartfelt gratefulness for the sound sleep
Every night without fail you offer me to sweep away
All filth of anxieties from weary mind far away.

71. Inside Out

A person known from knowledge he gained
Knowledge from the depth of things trained
Emotions come out from core of heart
Unveils the truth of eternity to impart
Aroma of musk from deer's navel
The more you explore when more places you travel
Happiness lies inside the heart of pain
Unless you suffer, yourself you can never nurture
Rising and falling, falling and raising both a mixture.

72. Existence

Children blindly believe in
Mother is a mother
Incomparable, unparallel
Unconditional in character
Nature and behavior
Students impulsively trust
Teachers as facilitator
Profound mender, mentor
Worldwide explorer, presenter
A maker of professional career
Passengers wholeheartedly count on
Driver as a safe carrier
Skilled holder to steer
The safety journey
Clients hopefully rely on
Pleaders for win to cheer
Patients entirely treat
Doctors as Messiah the Savior
The five reshapers of future.
Why not we ween others
Without being a betrayer
To sustain the existence
Of beautiful creation
Made by the Creator?
Believe in you

Before believe in others
To let things go
In their own way
The world will exist
Without going astray.

73. Rumination

Human heart loaded with
Thoughts of mist and myth
Some captures from inside
Some from outside breath.
Dive into depth of anything
Detract us from something
To attract the ones ever untold
Hidden truth exclusively explored.
Rumination moulds and reshapes man
From a stage of common to uncommon
From darkness to illumination
A call for worldwide reformation.
Sadness discharges the ray of joy
Just a means of life to enjoy
The pleasure of victory
Unfurling the cover of mystery.

74. Her Unknown Destiny

The pleasure of family ripples
Advent of a daughter sparkles
Hearts exult merrily bubbles
Moment of rapture rules
Strife somehow cripples.
Grows like crescent moon
Day by day time unknown
Call her lovely princess
My life', parents address.
Flowers like soft and tender
As fragrant as hidden musk
Swings in air without ponder
Hide and seek dawn to dusk.
Wheel of Time never stops
Changes steadily turn up
In persons places get up
Attitude look make up.
The journey of life starts
To her unknown destiny
Daughter to daughter-in-law
Searching identity in vicinity
Hopes are uncountable
Wants are indescribable
Dreams are surmountable
But sleepless nights feeble.

Time plays foul games with her
Captivated in the net of torture
The known remain unknown
Forlorn smiles no more return.
Her silence her strength
Suppressed fire of wrath
Centre of attraction collapsed
Joy of celebration lapsed.

75. Life Without You

Never felt the impact of any sorrow
The sunset of my life never seen in horizon's furrow
Never stood in the sun except the shadow
Night hides her face in the hollow
Never felt ever the pain of extreme hunger
Never faced any kind of physical or mental danger
Knew not the dearth of thirst any longer.
Because you both were with me to provide
Anything wished reached me from your side.
Everything looked beautiful and lively
Everything seemed colorful and homely
Everyday watched the rainbow of joy merrily
Everyday got I a message from morning crazily
Without any break up time passed easily
Never guessed any season except spring happily.
Because you were with me to expose the sight
Light of my life, soul of my life and heart of my life.
But time and my fate jealous of my happiness
Took away, both of you, my parents leaving me in loneliness
Today understood how painful my life without you
Counting days and nights nothing remains even a few
Everything was available and cheap in your presence
But the reverse here I see in your absence.

76. Crying In The Rain

Crying in the rain constant
Take away my pain distant
Putting out my fire instant
Of surreptitious desire.
Crying in the pain perfectly
Pleasure I gain secretly
Never comes again exactly
Slackness to slain recklessly
Weakness out to drain cautiously.
Crying in the rain continuous
Rains to reframe precious
Makes me solemn obvious
Secure my domain fabulous
Paradise regained joyous.
Crying in the rain steadily
Body drenched thoroughly
Heart dampened slightly
Mind sustained gently.

77. Service Begets Peace

Worldwide issue Kovid 19 Pandemic trembled innumerable hearts
No place under the sun remained untouched and unhurt
The mass panic at the situation severely felt unsafe
When emerged some brave hearts myriads lives to save.
Doctors like angels assuage the pain of fright
Police subdued crowd to stay home all right
With food volunteers rushing the spot as spotlight
A moment dedicated service and awareness to highlight.
Service to mankind in any form however concise
Begets eternal peace letting everyone to realize
Patently service the mighty power people to humanize
Devoted service only ensures the mortals to immortalize.

78. Truth Triumphs At Last

Lies and truth two sides of human life

Sometimes no escape from both sites.

Since time immemorial they exist

More or less for survival they conflict.

Dominance of lies over truth a habitual fashion

Truth only triumphs as God there to ransom.

At times mighty forces before lies admit

For the betterment of mankind to persist.

Lies and truth quite distinct

Where glass and where diamond instinct.

79. The Ideal Family

Not a group of members a family, a place of togetherness with
sameness
A laboratory of experimenting theory of nobility humility and
newness.
Not a place of living together extension of helping hands each other
A window to the world community exposure to gather further and
farther.
A factory where manufactured unique product of faith loyalty rapport
With branded quality ensured guarantee and good conduct import.
A nursing home to teach how to care regard and understand nature
Children, parents, younger elder older in respective of caste creed
colour.
A hub of sharing pain and pleasure without expectations
No fright of doubts, betrayal, lies and hallucinations.
A stage to perform diverse roles time to time assigned
With commitment, unity and integrity being self realized.
An altar to sacrifice quarrels desires monopolies diversity
To establish love peace kindness forgiveness serenity.
A lovely garden having flowers of beauty
To world wide spread the fragrance of humanity.
The ideal family a shrine of universal sublimity divinity
Enlightened with the light of equality, justice, and fraternity.
A heaven of cooperation, understanding, compromise and
adjustment
Where life cheerful purposeful meaningful enjoyment.

80. Coming Back Vs Setting Back

The old are out when the new in advent

When the attention goes to the present.

Moment of rapture plays hide and seek

After the old fall sick.

As the present is truth, felt and seen

Setting back loser the attachment.

Coming back always comes with novelty

How one can stay in the oblivion of serenity.

81. If You Stop Trying

Life is always moving across ups and downs
Failures and success, construction and destruction
On the way to destination.
In every walk of life failure comes
But not as adopted systems
Incessant effort on target defeats failures
If you focus on action, it can never allure
Failures are revised to get refined
Chances of getting faded ruined
Invigorating to come with flying colours
Drives you pile awards and honors'
Under the feet of Endeavour
Each moment becomes the boon to recover.
If you stop trying, failures will rob your all
Leaving you crying, repenting on your downfall
More you fall, more you rise if you keep on trying
Rest will be yours on the stage of life.

82. You Can

Today is the maker of tomorrow
What is done today preserved for tomorrow
You is the master builder in you
You can make, you can break too
You is ruler, controller, anchor of future
Coz, you is the reason of what you think
You is the reflection of what you wink
Miss not today to control your future
You is the mixture of better feature
Yes you can change, reshape and mould own career
You are the sole authority of yours to rear and cheer.

83. My Youth Days

Days are gone still remains fresh
Youth days of adolescence graced with might
Mockery, caricature, fun enticed
Days passed with flying delight.
Streams of promises flew incessant
Intoxicated as if a drunken peasant
Toiling days and nights over confident
Moments were so glorious and pleasant.
Broke the walls of impossibility with hammer's blow
Radiant are the wills and eagerness glow
Standing for the revered personality
Influenced a lot on me to proceed with agility.

84. Revenge

Going out of humanity
Men can forget identity
Inviting own downfall
Loses human capacity.
Everything goes wrong
Death bell is soon rung
Honesty is simply loosed
The whole world hushed.
Emerges intolerance in revenge
Patience is so tense to avenge
Speaking nonsense for advantage
Reactions influence without privilege.

85. Job

Every job is easy if one embraces
Different from places to places
Different from persons to persons
If there is passion, teaches great lessons.
Every job is great in its own place
We don't know the value unless we face
In every job there's His grace
Never underrate without realizing the base.
Job is no value for those who refrain
Everywhere they only do complain.

86. Being Alone Is Not Easy

• 91 •

To be alone is one type of punishment
Separation of relatives in spite of attachment
Unstable is mind to scatter here and there
When nobody is there to few words share.
Life is helpless in the absence of near and dear
Preoccupied mind indecisive in fear.
Loneliness takes away joy and happiness
A moment of anxiety losing consciousness
A place of nothingness to attract heart
Life becomes senseless as if five senses fall apart.

87. Kindness Can Change Lives

O kindness how you change
All of a sudden stop revenge
Where you come I don't know
Under your feet enemies bow
Heart of stone melts away
In the swing of joy sway.
Mind of negativity and narrowness widened
In your caress poems of your glory are penned
Desert of civilization turns to oasis
Thou are the messenger of divine bliss
O kindness, how you are so magnanimous
So kind and so wondrous.

88. Repeated Mistakes

• 93 •

To err is human
Inevitable in domain
Chances are there
To rectify it is fair
Perfection cares
When conscious we are
But repeat is a decision
Because of rigidness in action
In various occasions.

89. Can't Hurt Me

Not necessary to hurt
Unless something sought
Let life treat one and all
Because we are equal.
Once hurt never recovers
Leaving a scar forever
Reflects what we are
Before doing take care.

90. Why We Do

For livelihood to maintain the family
Do education to understand the situation
For betterment of society to progress
Reasons are innumerable to trace.
Something done for pleasure
Something for universal knowledge
Every deed has significance
Actions tell us how to survive.

91. Built To Serve

• 96 •

Everything born or created has a purpose
Serving more or less conscious or unconscious
Let you serve without hesitation
Each one here a beautiful creation.
Water to quench the thirst
To clean many a dirt
Making life comfort
Life cannot exist sans it.
Fire to consume the unwanted
To dress costumes habituated.
Rivers to take away with other rivulets
Vast seas to accommodate.

92. Win The Day

Greet with love fills the gap
In between winning and the winners
Do the best ignoring whether looser or gainer
Think good of others, the Almighty think of you
Someone think of you if you think of other
The day will be yours to win with flying colors
You understand what I mean to explore.
Be free and fair in your action
Which will offer you gratification
Even in your destitution
The end will be yours with aspiration.
Win the day with honesty and integrality
Sustaining humanity and fraternity.

93. Love Rules

Love makes us listen
As everywhere glisten
Felt, however unseen
No matter what can mean.
Love makes one understand
Situation to comprehend
Nothing to apprehend
But always takes stand.
Love makes one feel
Teaches how to deal
Knows what to fill
A lot it can reveal.
Love makes one render
Works as mender
No discrimination in gender
How it works I ponder.

94. Success Is Sum Of Small Efforts

Not the result of luxury and comfort
Sum total of small, smaller or the smallest efforts
Fruits of hard labour and incessant sweat
Series of many a failures and attempts.
Daring steps to dream for the world community
Without being a dare devil to ruin the society
Courage to face any sort of adversity
Harvesting the crops of fertility.

95. Mistakes Are Opportunities

Mistakes are golden opportunities to retry
Avail without losing, without cry.
Mistakes are revision for perfections
Drive away all your imperfections.
Mistakes are kind hearted to give another chance
To explore, open the gate of entrance.
Mistakes are encouragement to proceed
Admit, embrace with live and sacrifice to supersede.
Mistakes are teachers to rectify the errors
Not barriers but pave the way of career.
Mistakes are researchers to find the right
Afraid not let them do, support them without fight.
Mistakes explore the arena of newness and accuracy
Extend your helping hands with enthusiasm and intimacy.
Mistakes plough the land of hardcore futility
With hope and trust to bring back fertility.

96. National Energy Conservation Day

A day of celebration
A day of observation
For awareness creation
For energy conservation
Divine work of humanization.
Loss of energy loss of human society
Thus not a day but days are necessity
Promises to keep for eternity
Welfare of the whole world community
Let people do something for own posterities.
If one does wrong is injustice to all
Indirectly inviting own downfall
Conservation of energy leading humanity
Let's work for the worldwide solidarity.

97. Silence

Silence in silence
Speaks in abundance
Unspeakable credence
Suppression of intolerance
Creates miracles
Crossing the bar of obstacles.
Silence though indifference
To other's benevolence
Ocean of patience and perseverance
Holding the pearls of opulence.
Heart of silence stores nostalgia
Sometimes works as panacea
The way to the realm of divinity
Opens the gate of creativity.
All solutions to confronted problems
Manifested inside the core of silence
Vividness with lucidity sparkles
Enlightening the heart forever.

98. Pray, Trust, Wait

Praying a power of communicating
The Almighty in all situations to tackle
Gives strength to fight for the right
In prayer mind forever delights.
Prayer is a trust to believe in God's grace
Emerging as a savior life to refresh
Prayer and trust makes a bridge to join
To understand the link between creator and creation.
Everything needs a time of its own
Waiting and watching ends the test alone
As nothing happens neither before nor after
Useless to be in helter-skelter.

99. Change Is Necessary

Anything born destined to change
Nothing remains constant
However uncomfortable and painful
Changes necessary to make life cheerful
Change is the law of nature
No powers stop flow of water.
Change is inevitable to grow
Growth moves life to flow
No change, no life lives
Magnificent gifts a change leaves.

100. Be Free, Be True, Be You

You are everything
But something missing
Be free for exploring
Be true for inspiring
Be you aspiring
Let the world rejoice
But yours is the choice.
Be you what you are
Control your desire
To control the fire
Everything you are.

101. Never Be An Option

Everything you have to challenge
Without taking any revenge
Everything you have to use
Why then think of ugly misuse?
Everything you have to compete
Before fight, fear not for defeat
Thou are the only potion, not an option
Fit yourself in every situation.
Let you be the only choice
Let life rejoice even in menace
Thou are being the sources of solace
Let others not harass or regress
You are all in all to refresh
Let me pray to the Almighty to grace.
For making you a man of prudence
Abounds in self confidence and credence.

102. Everything Has Its Own Time

What burns is meant to grow

What grows takes time to mature

Nature's rule to follow, not to lampoon

Everything has its own time to croon

As in the cerulean azure the silvery moon.

Between morn and evening, noon and afternoon.

Seasons emerge one after the other

Like six sisters from one mother

Culture and customs of Nature

Reigning over own time, ones power

Being potential in order to nurture

The whole universe in rapture.

As a day takes twelve hours to live

After twelve hours of rest morning peeps

Before which it can't cleave, even though grieve

Pain and pleasure appears to be friend

None can stay in other's absence, unable to brief

Time anchors everything in silence without peeve.

103. Listen To Your Heart

Believe not what you hear
What you hear may not be true
As things are not what they seem
Heart is our own to beam
Better listen to the heart not to others
There's no question to bother
When heart is with you to preview.
No stress and strain to review
Heart speaks what you wish
In every moment of divine bliss
Heart can never betray you in abyss
Always guides like a mother's kiss
That drizzles open you love and pace
To suffice your life, never miss
Everything you have, do furnish
For the right decision to accomplish.

104. Some Losses Set You Free

Loss is to gain
Though gives pain
Mankind, it does train
Without any problem.
Some losses set you free
To march forward in glee
Generous like a tree
Fair and blair unlatching life mystery
Never count open losses
That makes you flourish
Or repent upon missing
Leaving you promising.
Everything has two sights to move on
Without one the other never goes on.

105. Life Without Action

Life be vagabond without actions
Heart be cheerless without emotions
Mind be hard without thoughts
Body be a log without hurts.
Life without action meaningless
Words without meaning useless
Action without devotion aimless
Thought without logic shapeless.
Actions make life active and energetic
Removing slackness traumatic
Alluring each nerve and cell dynamic
For the purpose of humanity aesthetic.

106. Some Souls Suffer Silently

Soul knows everything
Hidden nothing unknown
For others, some souls suffer
Want not anybody to hamper
Takes time to pardon with fine temper
Even if abandoned lonely forever.
Unseen are the souls that cry
The rivers of tears never dry
Everything in motion can fly
But soul never becomes sly.
For the sake of the best, hold
Some souls carol the song untold
Hearts are kept awake by loud load
Discernible the scrape in many folds
But mix-up can never withhold.

107. Pleasure And Freedom For Pain

Freedom gives pleasure
Pleasure gives treasure
Treasure your treasure
Never ever measure.
Pain is absolutely heavier
But changes behavior
Helps shedding tears
The end bestows cheers.
Pain ends with gain
Forever remain
Tasted and tested
Nowhere to complain.

108. Listener

Listening an art of patience
Listener a calm drawee of attention
To listen is to instill power of perseverance
Act of goodness for future retention.
Being listener nourishes mind
Potion with rightness and accuracy
Being human leave something behind
Impression will impress to shine in ecstasy.
Better to listen before you speak
Otherwise you cannot reach the peak
Judge not in a peek like a pique
Effective listening verses how to pick
And most importantly what to speak.

109. Push Yourself

Not all doors are open to enter
Some are closed with gutter
Unless you push nobody will open
Endeavour is kept on and on.
Things do not come to you
By force in due in a queue
Football never rolls down
Unless you kick, it does not whirl round.
Push yourself to the arena difficulties
You can overcome all adversities
Easily you can reach necessities
With increasing abilities.
Human life is what you wish to shape
Environment makes life to save
From what you do or what you have.
The rest becomes as to what you behave.

110. Less Ego, More Soul

No peace in
Wealth accumulated.
No loss in
Wisdom circulated.
No love in
Heartless heart.
Fewer egos more soul
More egos, more sore.
No freedom in
Excess command of control
In no register of life, enroll
To obtain the testimony of pure sole.

111. Be Nice, But Learn To Say No

Saying no to injustice
Gives that divine bliss.
Saying no to bad deeds
Happily everybody feeds.
Saying no to hatred
Never can betray.
Everything is fairly nice
When one gets his price.
If you say, no to corruption
You can stay in gratification.
Far away from vice
And be nice to entice.

112. Protect My Energy

Need to help the poor
Wish to share my all
Want all do the best
So protect my energy
To stand for allergy.
Let my eyes see the good
My nose smell the fragrance of loving mood
My hand to toil for feeding
My mind to capture the finest for inspiring.
Promise to keep my commitment
Delighted to see other achievement
Try my level best to help the helpless
Oh, God protect my energy with your grace.

113. Accept The Situation

Stop not the journey
Situations come and go
Face it, moves ahead
Destination, it will show.
Occurrence or happenings
Never come informing
But inevitable to appear
Let it play its role
Keep travel heart and soul.
Be bold and accept the situation
Amidst failures and victory
Time will show the destination
The rest will be history.

114. My Failures

My failures my negligence
Ignoring of diligence
Lack of endeavors and confidence
Reasons of my failures in abundance
Deceiving own self is deceiving other
Refraining from hard work always bother
Indifference to devotion and action
Invites at last own destruction.
My failures the result of my action
Action without proper ambition
Which takes one away from destination
Making friends with failures by heart
Definitely help in time of depression
Failures, first time, is supposed to test my valour
Unless I embrace it can never allure me galore.

115. Don't Quit

Life is to move
Hang not on groove
But full of assignments
For rendering achievements
Half done is not done
Never try to abandon
Stick to duty and promises
Till last breath of life to access
For sure success, time will asses.
Life is not meant for quit
Unless and until you fit
Leave not the work for defeat
Don't think you are unfit
Keep on effort to pick bit by bit
And employ your wit and conceit.

116. Sometimes Some Moments

Sometimes some moments of rapture
Like a camera mind often do capture.
Sometimes some moments so valuable
Each moment of life highly discernible.
Sometimes some moments so priceless
When humans are not more reckless.
Sometimes some moments so caring
Under which like becomes inspiring.
Sometimes some moments memorable
Fresh and lively, spontaneously movable.
Sometimes some moments very near and dear
Stop shedding tears rather makes life cheer.

117. Be Kind To Yourself

If you are kind, you can never mind
If you never mind, you will be happy, remind.
Life is what you make, and what you do
In return you can receive what you perceive.
If you are kind, everything will be meaningful
No underestimation, no discrimination
Life will be more beautiful and cheerful
Without any illusion, without hallucinations.
If you are kind you will see one and all so kind
You will get what you are in mind.
Since kindness can win the hearts of mankind
Nothing will remain blank the curtain behind
Be kind to yourself, kindness is your pelf
If you make yourself whelve.

118. Patience And Motivation

Patience
Foundation of the edifice of life
Drinks the water of all human strife
Struggle without patience certainly vain
Patience sows the seeds of ultimate gain.
Have the foundation of love and peace
Patience will tender you eternal bliss.
Motivation
Life can never move without motivation
It ensures and inspires for concentration
Drives to the world of positivity
To harvest the crops of fertility.
Motivation gives energy to carry on life's journey
Showering open you the blessed harmony.

119. Ego

Excess stupidity
Too much gravity
Showing superiority
Dearth of humility.
False pride to show
A man of saying no
Inability to follow
Remains as hollow.
An empty vessel
Building castles
In the air to dare
Feeling awkward to share.

120. Discipline

Doorways to goal paved
When discipline swayed
Contemplation rises to culmination
Destination comes closer with sensation
Time and space well exploited
To reach the reach out even depressed.
Discipline makes a man a noble man
Erasing everything bad to make him main
Enables each and every one inquisitive to train
Widening the scope of brain to remain
As the shining star in the sky of human
Sometimes the moon among the stars.

121. Meditation

Concentration in silence units all senses
Garners wisdom from even commonsense
Mingling in the world of positivity mind explores
The distant horizon in different colours.
Scattering mind gets together in meditation
Courage and knowledge right combination
To sail the boards of life in the river of consolation
With the power of isolation and toleration.
Problems of life are solved with quick solution
When one remains in haven of meditation
Enlightenment he/she gets in contemplation
Finding the underline truth of define creation
Meditation a panacea to all evil of society.
A key to the realization of humanity
A moment of opportunities to get emancipation
From all the chains of human hallucination.

122. Murky Seren Night

Two souls in search of a murky seren night to mingle each other
That ensures their meeting safe and free of cacophony
The lonely sea shore or outskirts of crowd ecstatic seeing the
confluence
Multiplies the much awaited dreams of life, one another influence.
Twinkling stars in the azure sky showering flowers of blessings
Gelid wind whistling piercing but quite appealing
Rushing sound of serenity in loneliness lustrous heart oozing.
Moonlit busy preparing velvety rosy bed perfume spreading.
Time, space, place splendidly comprehends lover's emotions
Spell of love makes each other insane in collaboration.

123. Tough Situations

Life is amalgam of ups and downs
Prosperity and adversity
But tough situations make life stronger
Moulding those facing boldly as rangers
It provides courage and energy
To keep efforts on for growth and development
Gives power of stamina to hold the load of bravery
Opening the gate of all obscurity and mystery.

124. Try Again Better

Nobody is perfect from his birth
Nothing is perfect from its creation
It is the efforts that make one able
It is the revisions that make something possible
Loser is he who does not try again
Incessant endeavour can solve any problem
Continuous falling of water on a piece of stone
Makes it soften to break into pieces
Regular walking on foot unleashes green grass or bush
A clean way is formed on the passage of time.
Trying again and again enables to defeat
What cannot be done only once be possible in repeat.

125. Time Is Powerful

Time changes everything
Spares nobody or nothing
Time brings chilly winter to ruin
So does spring, newness to coin
With the passing of time runs the rivulet
Widened the river and vast sea to accommodate
Dark clouds to clean the cerulean sky
Transparent the scene, the sun rises high.
Men of penury can rise to the gallery of opulence
Houseful of confluence, sure to vacate in silence
If time can break you, it can heal you too
So don't look down upon time as fool
Neither you miss nor can you befoul.